Baseball in April and Other Stories

by
Gary Soto

Teacher Guide

Written by
Monica L. Odle

Note

The Harcourt paperback edition, © 1990 by Gary Soto, was used to prepare this guide. The page references may differ in other editions. ISBN: 0-15-202567-7

Please note: Please assess the appropriateness of these books for the age level and maturity of your students prior to reading and discussing the texts with them.

ISBN: 978-1-60539-008-6

Copyright infringement is a violation of Federal Law.

© 2008 by Novel Units, Inc., Bulverde, Texas. All rights reserved. No part of this publication may be reproduced, translated, stored in a retrieval system, or transmitted in any way or by any means (electronic, mechanical, photocopying, recording, or otherwise) without prior written permission from ECS Learning Systems, Inc.

Photocopying of student worksheets by a classroom teacher at a non-profit school who has purchased this publication for his/her own class is permissible. Reproduction of any part of this publication for an entire school or for a school system, by for-profit institutions and tutoring centers, or for commercial sale is strictly prohibited.

Novel Units is a registered trademark of ECS Learning Systems, Inc.
Printed in the United States of America.

To order, contact your local school supply store, or—
Novel Units, Inc.
P.O. Box 97
Bulverde, TX 78163-0097

Web site: www.novelunits.com

Table of Contents

General Overview 3

About the Author 3

Initiating Activities 4

Vocabulary Activities 5

Eleven Sections (Stories) 6
    Each section contains: Summary, Characters, Vocabulary,
    Discussion Questions, and Supplementary Activities

Post-reading Discussion Questions 23

Post-reading Extension Activities 24

Assessment 25

Scoring Rubric 32

Skills and Strategies

Thinking
Research, critical thinking, decision making, compare/contrast

Comprehension
Predicting, cause/effect, evaluating decisions, summarization

Writing
Journal, poetry, short story, summary, letter, character sketch

Listening/Speaking
Discussion, oral presentation, acting/drama

Vocabulary
Definitions, parts of speech, pronunciation, antonyms, glossary

Literary Elements
Conflict, irony, universal themes, figurative language, point of view, characterization, setting, genre

Across the Curriculum
Science—gears, conducting electricity; Health/Sports—baseball, karate; History—Confederate money; Music—guitar; Foreign Languages—Spanish, French; Art—caricature, diorama

Genre: short stories

Setting: lower-class neighborhoods of Fresno, California

Style: narrative; third-person omniscient

Tone: lighthearted, fun, often humorous

Themes: coming-of-age, race, culture, love, friendship, success/failure, life's lessons, self-discovery

Conflict: person vs. self, person vs. person, person vs. society

Date of First Publication: 1990

General Overview

In this novel, Gary Soto explores universal issues of young adolescents through the stories of 11 Latino teenagers growing up in Fresno, California. Through the children's stories, the reader is granted access to their world, experiencing the trials associated with the pre-teen and teenage years. This collection of stories provides an insider's understanding of the frustrations suffered and triumphs enjoyed through the experience of everyday juvenile activities, such as playing baseball, riding a bike, shooting marbles, or playing with Barbie dolls.

About the Author

Gary Soto was born on April 12, 1952, in Fresno, California, the second of three children born to Manuel and Angie Soto. He grew up in one of the city's *barrios*, or lower-class neighborhoods. When Soto was five years old, his father died in an accident while working at the Sun-Maid Raisin Company. Growing up in a culture of poverty, excellence in education was not something Soto pursued or achieved in childhood. He did, however, begin developing a love of reading by spending time in the school library. He attended Fresno College for two years after graduating high school. It was there that Soto discovered poetry. After two years, he transferred to California State University at Fresno where he took his first poetry class and studied under Philip Levine. Soto received a B.A. in English from California State University and an M.A. in Creative Writing from the University of California at Irvine. In 1975, he married Carolyn Oda. The couple had one daughter, Mariko Heidi. In 1977, Soto began teaching Chicano studies at the University of California at Berkeley where he continued teaching until 1993. Besides writing and teaching, Soto is also the Young People's Ambassador for the United Farm Workers of America and California Rural Legal Assistance. He currently lives in Berkeley, California.

Gary Soto's writing career began with his first book of poetry, *The Elements of San Joaquin*, published in 1977. His second volume of poetry, *The Tale of Sunlight*, was published in 1978 and nominated for the Pulitzer Prize. Soto has since written many novels, volumes of poetry, and short stories for people of all ages. Among his many awards and honors are the Literature Award from the Hispanic Heritage Foundation as well as the Author-Illustrator Civil Rights Award from the National Education Association. *Baseball in April and Other Stories*, published in 1990, was Soto's first work for children. It won the California Library Association's Beatty Award and was named an ALA Best Book for Young Adults. Soto continues to write and publish today.

Initiating Activities

1. Genre: As a class, use the Venn diagram on page 26 of this guide to brainstorm the differences between a novel and a short story. What literary elements are common and unique to both genres of writing?

2. Brainstorming: Using the Pros and Cons chart on page 27 of this guide, write "middle school student" at the top. Allow students to brainstorm the pros and cons of being a middle school student.

3. Writing: Have students write a short story about an event that might occur in a day in the life of a young teenager.

4. Prediction: Ask students to think about the title of the book, *Baseball in April and Other Stories*, and predict what the book will be about.

5. Diversity/Universality: Each of the book's short stories focuses on different Latino young adults. As such, aspects of Latino culture are part of each of the main characters' lives. Discuss how people of all races, ethnicities, or cultures can relate to a book whose main characters are a part of one specific culture. Then discuss the benefits of reading books about people from a variety of cultures and backgrounds.

Vocabulary Activities

1. Vocabulary Strike Out: Define 20 vocabulary words. Write each definition on one side of a note card and the corresponding word on the back. Then post 25 words on the board, including in these the 20 words from the note cards, and adding five extra words. Divide the class into two groups. Each group will take turns listening to a definition and then guessing which word is being defined. For every incorrect guess, that team receives one X on the board indicating a strike. The first team to receive three strikes loses.

2. Vocabulary Sort and Sentences: Have students sort the vocabulary words into two columns—"words I use regularly" and "words I do not use often or at all." Students must then write a set of ten sentences. Each sentence must use at least one word from each column.

3. Vocabulary Tic-Tac-Toe: Select nine students to sit in three rows of three in the classroom. Give each student a large cut-out of an X and an O. Select two other students to compete. One student is "X," and the other is "O." Student X is asked to define a vocabulary word. S/he must choose one of the nine students sitting in a square to define the word, and then state whether s/he agrees or disagrees with the given definition. If Student X correctly agrees or disagrees with the given definition, the sitting student must display the X. If Student X incorrectly agrees or disagrees, the sitting student displays the O. Alternate turns between Students X and O. The first student to have three Xs or Os in a row (vertical, horizontal, or diagonal) wins.

4. Word Quilt: Each student chooses a vocabulary word from the book. Using different colors of paper, have the students create unique squares to represent the words they chose. Each square should include at least three of the following: definition, part of speech, a simile, pronunciation, an antonym, a sentence, an illustration, or a quote from the book. Finally, have students paste the squares together on a larger square sheet of paper. Display this "word quilt" in the classroom.

5. Glossary: Instruct students to keep a list of any unfamiliar or difficult words they encounter as they read the book. Students will create a glossary from their lists. Glossaries should include each word's pronunciation, part of speech, and definition as it is used in the text. (Students may include Spanish words or phrases in their glossary. Remind them that a glossary for Spanish terms is provided in the back of the book and can be used as a resource.)

"Broken Chain"

Alfonso is smitten with Sandra, a girl in his grade at school. He invites her to go bike riding with him but spends the week worrying about how he will find a bike for Sandra to ride. After his own bike chain breaks, he worries even more about disappointing the girl he likes—until his older brother comes to his rescue.

Genre: short story, young-adult fiction

Setting: Central Valley of California

Point of View: third-person omniscient

Themes: family, love, acceptance, self-image, coming-of-age

Conflict: person vs. person, person vs. self

Tone: conversational, informative

Characters

Alfonso: self-conscious seventh-grade boy who finds himself interested in a neighbor girl his age

Ernie: Alfonso's older brother

Sandra: girl who captures Alfonso's attention

Frankie: Sandra's little brother

Raymundo: Ernie's friend

Vocabulary
apparent
sullen
winced
stunt
impulse
sprocket
emerged

Discussion Questions

1. What are two things that Alfonso does to improve his appearance? Why do you think he does these things? (*Pushes on his teeth to make them straight, does sit-ups to make his abs look "cut," gets his hair cut flat on top; To feel good about himself and to impress others*)

2. Without expressly saying it, how does the author tell readers the general social class to which Alfonso's family belongs? Do you think the author's methods are effective or not? Explain. (*The author talks about the boys' bicycles being from Montgomery Ward, the family not having enough money to get braces for Alfonso, the girls that Ernie likes being poor as evidenced by their choice of Halloween costume, etc; The author's methods are very effective. The reader can tell that the family has enough money to survive and even has a few luxuries, like bicycles and high-top shoes, but they are not wealthy.*)

3. Why is it important for an author to establish facts about main characters very early in a short story? (*Short stories are, by definition, short, and most of the story will revolve around a conflict. In order for the story to make an impact, readers need a quick understanding of the major character[s] and conflict. A short story must do what a novel would do, but in less time, and that is to immediately develop a major character while putting the story's plot in motion.*)

4. A "meet-cute" is the way in which two characters who are attracted to each other meet. What situation does the author create to introduce Sandra to Alfonso? (*Alfonso is riding his*

bike when he sees a young boy hanging from a fence. He stops to help the boy down and finds he is the younger brother of a girl in his class, Sandra, whom Alfonso finds attractive. Sandra is grateful that she doesn't have to tell her mother that her little brother is stuck on a fence, and Sandra and Alfonso begin a conversation.)

5. What conflict arises for Alfonso after asking Sandra to go bike-riding with him? What type of conflict is this? (*Alfonso must convince his brother, Ernie, to let him borrow his bicycle for the hour of his "date" with Sandra since Sandra's bike has a flat. Ernie doesn't want to let Alfonso borrow it; Person vs. person*)

6. Why does Ernie suspect that the girl going on a date with his brother is the same girl who stood him up? Do you think Ernie's assumption is valid? Why or why not? (*She lives two blocks from where the other girls told Ernie to meet them, she is in the correct grade, and she wears her hair in ponytails. Ernie's assumptions are not really valid since none of these details are factual evidence. There are probably several girls that live in a two-block radius of the meeting spot, wear ponytails, and are in the seventh grade.*)

7. What is ironic about Alfonso's bike chain breaking? (*Alfonso takes much better care of his bike than his brother, cleaning and maintaining it on a regular basis. However, while caring for his bike, the chain breaks so that he cannot ride the bike. At the same time, his brother's dirty, unkempt bike works fine.*)

8. What do you predict will happen when Alfonso shows up at Sandra's house without even one bicycle? (*Answers will vary.*)

9. What does it say about Ernie when he lets Alfonso borrow his bike? (*It shows that Ernie was able to overcome some of his jealousy about Alfonso having a girlfriend and proves that he does care about Alfonso.*)

Supplementary Activities

1. Figurative Language: Figurative language conveys meaning through the use of analogy. Begin making a list of the figurative language in the novel. Examples: **Similes**—"sit…sullen as a toad" (p. 2); "his teeth were crooked, like a pile of wrecked cars" (p. 2); "his [bike] gleamed like a handful of dimes" (p. 4); "chain lay in his hand like a dead snake" (p. 9); "chain…slicing his hand like a snake's fang" (p. 9); "trudging slowly, as if he were waist-deep in water" (p. 10)

2. Journal: Think of your own short story idea. In your journal, write a "meet-cute" for two people who will become a couple later in your story.

3. Poetry: Write a descriptive poem about how you think Sandra feels riding on the crossbar of Ernie's bike while Alfonso pedals.

4. Science: Research how a bicycle works. Draw a diagram of the gears, and present your findings to the class.

"Baseball in April"

Two brothers, Michael and Jesse, try out and fail to make the local Little League team. Though discouraged, the boys decide to join a neighborhood team with a nice coach. Though there are only two teams in the league and the boys' team loses every game, Jesse continues to play through the end of the season.

Genre: short story, young-adult fiction

Setting: Fresno, California

Point of View: third-person omniscient

Themes: rejection, courage, values

Conflict: person vs. person, person vs. self

Tone: informative, matter of fact

Characters

Jesse: 9-year-old who tries out for the Little League baseball team; not a great player but loves the game

Michael: Jesse's older brother; encouraging; good at baseball

Manuel: middle-aged, fatherly coach of the Hobos baseball team

Vocabulary
nonchalantly
reassurance
furrowed

Discussion Questions

1. What can you tell about Michael and Jesse's relationship based on how they treat each other during Little League tryouts? (*Michael and Jesse are nice to each other, and Michael, though older and a better baseball player, is kind and encouraging to his little brother. They seem good-natured and determined.*)

2. Why do you think the author chooses to write the story so that both boys do not make the Little League team? How would the story have been different if Michael had made the team and Jesse had not? (*The brothers are able to stay together for the rest of the story since Michael doesn't make the team. His true colors shine when he quits the Hobos because he has a girlfriend. Jesse's stamina is further illustrated when he keeps playing with the Hobos for the entire season, even after his brother, who clearly has more talent, quits the team. Answers will vary.*)

3. Manuel serves as a father figure to many of the boys on his team. Does he seem to be a good father figure? (*Manuel seems to be a good father figure because he is patient and kind. He seems to care about the kids he coaches, and playing with them is more about building a team and having fun than winning. Also, many of the children on the team don't have father figures at all, so Manuel may be one of the only adult men from whom they can learn about sports and competition.*)

4. What is the significance of the team name "the Hobos"? (*All of the players did not make it into the more prestigious league, so they have to settle for a team with no uniforms or fancy field. Rather than a real season, they simply practice and play one other team repetitively. In a way, it is a team of castaways or misfits.*)

5. Do you think it was a good or bad decision for Michael and Jesse to join the Hobos? What might have kept them from joining the team? (*Answers will vary, but note that Jesse does improve his skills by being part of the team and having a coach, opportunities he would not have had if he hadn't joined the team. Making the Little League team would have prevented the brothers from joining the team. Also, pride could have kept them from joining the team, but their humility gains them an opportunity to play a game they love.*)

6. Which brother likes to play baseball more? Why do you think so? (*Michael is older and better at the game and could be considered the one who loves the game more, but he doesn't care much about playing after he doesn't make the Little League team. Jesse is younger and not as good as his older brother, but he sticks with the Hobos for the entire season until Manuel no longer shows up to coach.*)

Supplementary Activities

1. Figurative Language: Continue adding to your list. Examples: **Similes**—"number flapped like a broken wing" (p. 14); "smaller kids were in awe of the paper number on his back…as if he were a soldier going off to war" (p. 15); "weighed the ball…like a pound of bologna" (p. 17)

2. Health/Sports: Research the rules of baseball and softball. Write a short essay, or design a visual aid to present to the class explaining the similarities and differences between the two sports.

3. Vocabulary: Make a list of all of the "baseball" words used in this short story. Using your list, create a glossary of terms. Remember to alphabetize the words when turning in your final copy.

"Two Dreamers"

Luis dreams of one day buying land in his neighborhood in Fresno, selling it for a profit, and retiring in Mexico as "El Millonario." Unfortunately, he must hide his plans from his disapproving wife and rely on his nine-year-old grandson, Hector, to help him with clandestine schemes.

Genre: short story, young-adult fiction

Setting: Fresno, California

Point of View: third-person omniscient

Themes: family, dreams, honesty

Conflict: person vs. person, person vs. self

Tone: conversational

Characters

Hector: nine-year-old boy who spends summers with his grandparents

Luis Molina: Hector's grandfather who has aspirations of buying and selling real estate to make money

Genaro: Luis' son-in-law who recently bought and sold a house for a decent profit

Grandma: Hector's grandmother; Luis' wife who does not approve of his money-making schemes

Vocabulary
craning
ambitious
stucco
assured
bickering
gusto

Discussion Questions

1. What kind of relationship do Hector and Luis seem to have? What qualities about each of them are factors in this relationship? (*They seem good-natured toward each other, and both seem to esteem the other for different reasons even though they are separated by an entire generation. Luis values his grandson's abilities to speak English and evaluate real estate costs, perhaps because Hector has grown up in the United States. Hector respects his grandfather's age and wisdom and feels very young and ignorant compared to the adults he deals with in the story.*)

2. Do you agree or disagree with Luis' wife that Luis should not think about buying a second house? Explain. (*Some may think she is being reasonable because they don't have enough money to buy a second house just to resell it. Others may think she is too harsh and that she should support her husband in his dream of taking a risk in order to become more financially secure.*)

3. Luis offers Hector money and a Confederate bill to call the realtor for him. Do you think it is worth it? Why doesn't Luis make the phone calls himself? (*Clearly, Luis doesn't get his money's worth on either phone call because Grandma's arrival cuts both calls short. By having Hector call the realtor, Luis feels more detached from the process. He knows his wife disapproves of the venture, so by not actually making the call, he is less liable for investigating the cost of the house that is for sale. Another reason Luis does not want to call could be that he feels intimidated talking to people who are native English speakers and may feel that his grandson can have a better English conversation because Hector was raised in America.*)

4. Do you think Luis will ever buy a house to resell? Why or why not? (*Answers will vary.*)

5. Discuss the significance of the title of the story. Who are the dreamers? What are their dreams? What are some of the obstacles they must face to achieve their dreams? (*Luis and Hector; Luis has a dream of retiring in Mexico as a rich man. However, he must overcome his wife's objections to some of his ideas about how to make money. Hector's dreams are less specific, but it is clear that he wants to get along with his grandfather and see his grandparents get along.*)

Supplementary Activities

1. Figurative Language: Continue adding to your list. Examples: **Similes**—"his dream went out like a lightbulb" (p. 28); "woman's gnat-like voice" (p. 28); "looked at the phone as if it were a thing she had never seen before" (p. 31)

2. Journal: In your journal, outline a dream you have. Write down a list of short-term and long-term goals you can work toward to achieve your dream. Also, write down a list of obstacles you might have to face when working toward your dream. Remember that sometimes things must be sacrificed to achieve dreams and also that sometimes a dream must be put on hold so that you can achieve other goals that are more urgent and of greater importance.

3. History: Luis gives his grandson a Confederate bill as bribery to make the telephone call to the realtor. Research what Confederate money looks like. Then determine how much money, if any, a 1,000 dollar Confederate bill is worth to collectors today.

"Barbie"

Veronica is disappointed by her uncle's gift of an imitation Barbie. The next year, her uncle arrives with his new fiancée, and the two of them present Veronica with a real Barbie. Veronica is elated and plays with her new doll with her friend Martha. On the way home from Martha's house, Veronica realizes Barbie's head is missing. In the end, Veronica is left with a damaged imitation Barbie and a headless real one, and she loves them both.

Genre: short story, young-adult fiction

Setting: Central Valley of California

Point of View: third-person omniscient

Themes: prejudice, irony, globalization

Conflict: person vs. person, person vs. self

Tone: descriptive, emotional

Characters

Veronica Solis: young girl who is disappointed that her uncle gave her an imitation Barbie but is later excited to receive an authentic one

Helen: Veronica's mother

Uncle Rudy: Veronica's uncle; gives her an imitation Barbie and then an authentic one a year later

Donna: Rudy's fiancée

Martha: Veronica's friend; tries to swap her Barbie doll with Veronica's

Vocabulary
imposter
sported
feigning
preoccupied
retraced

Discussion Questions

1. Veronica is very disappointed that she received an imitation Barbie from her uncle rather than an authentic one. Why do you think young girls feel that a Barbie doll is such a wonderful toy? Why is an imitation Barbie the "worst kind of doll" to Veronica (p. 34)? (*Young girls see Barbie dolls as the embodiment of female beauty. Girls don't want to pretend they are beautiful or almost beautiful; they want authentic beauty. The "worst kind of doll" is one that possesses only fake beauty, like the imitation Barbie.*)

2. After damaging her imitation doll, Veronica calls it "ugly." Do you think Barbie dolls represent beauty? If a Barbie is considered beautiful, does that make all other dolls ugly? Discuss the concept of beauty, especially as it relates to Barbie and other dolls. (*The image of beauty presented by Barbie dolls is very narrow and is itself an unrealistic portrayal of beauty. Barbie's physical measurements are impossible for a human woman to attain. If Barbie is considered beautiful, that does not make all other dolls ugly. Beauty is not something that can be concretely defined. Answers will vary.*)

3. Do you think people tend to value things that are beautiful more than things that are not? Why or why not? Do you think things that are beautiful inherently possess more value than things that are not as pretty? (*Some people may tend to assign more value to things that*

are beautiful than things that are not, just as Veronica believes a real Barbie is a better toy than the "ugly" imitation. While beautiful things may be pretty to look at, that does not mean they deserve more love than those things that are not beautiful. Beauty and significance are in the eyes of the beholder. Answers will vary.)

4. Do you think that Barbie losing her head is Martha's fault? (*No, Martha had nothing to do with Barbie's head falling off, and it was Veronica's decision to go play at Martha's house.*)

5. At the end of the story, Veronica has two damaged dolls. However, the Barbie doll is by far more damaged because her head is missing. What do you think Veronica has learned when you see her bring both dolls "lovingly to bed" (p. 42)? (*Veronica realizes that she loves both dolls because they are hers. Even without a head or an eyelash, the dolls belong to her, so she loves them. She seems to have learned that beauty is not just about the dolls' appearance but also about what she feels in her heart toward them.*)

Supplementary Activities

1. Figurative Language: Continue adding to your list. Example: **Simile**—"one of the eyelashes was peeling off like a scab" (p. 34)

2. Journal: In your journal, describe your favorite childhood toy and why it was your favorite.

"No Guitar Blues"

Fausto dreams of playing the guitar but knows that his family does not have the money to buy him one. In a desperate attempt, he returns a seemingly lost dog to its owners who live in a nice neighborhood, and he lies about finding the dog near the freeway. The couple shower Fausto with kindness and money. Fausto feels guilty about accepting the money due to telling a lie, so he gives it away to the church. Then his mother remembers seeing a bass guitarron in her father's garage, and Fausto begins to learn how to play the instrument from his grandfather.

Genre: short story, young-adult fiction

Setting: Central Valley of California

Point of View: third-person omniscient

Themes: dreams, shame, redemption, compassion, poverty

Conflict: person vs. self

Tone: descriptive, emotional

Characters

Fausto: young boy who dreams of playing the guitar on "American Bandstand" one day

Fausto's mother: will not promise to buy Fausto a guitar; later remembers seeing a guitarron in her father's garage

Helen: woman to whom Roger belongs; offers Fausto a turnover and insists Fausto take the money offered by her husband

Lawrence: Fausto's older brother

Grandfather Lupe: Fausto's grandfather; teaches Fausto to play the bass guitarron

Vocabulary
perpetual
vacant
deceitful
fidgeted
reluctantly
resounded

Discussion Questions

1. Do you think Fausto's dream of becoming a guitarist is a realistic one? Should he try to fulfill this dream? Explain why or why not. (*Answers will vary.*)

2. Do you think Fausto will be able to earn enough money to buy a guitar? (*Answers will vary.*)

3. Do you think Fausto should have lied to Roger's owners about where he found the dog? Why or why not? Discuss what is acceptable for someone to do while in pursuit of a dream. (*Fausto should not have lied to Roger's owners. Lying is not the best way for someone to get what he wants. Doing things with moral integrity will make a person's success sweeter. Doing things without good morals squelches the satisfaction of the achievement. Answers will vary.*)

4. Do you think Roger's owners believed Fausto's lie about finding the dog by the freeway? Why or why not? (*They probably do not believe the lie. They are not concerned that their dog isn't home that morning, which probably means that the dog roams the neighborhood often. They do, however, have compassion for Fausto and reward him anyway because they can see that he is a good-hearted child trying to earn a reward. Answers will vary.*)

5. Do you think Fausto does the right thing by giving the money to the church? Why or why not? (*Giving the money to the church is a good deed, and Fausto is able to relieve his guilt and shame for lying by giving the money away. Note that he ends up receiving exactly the kind of guitar he wants after he alleviates his guilt by admitting his lie and giving away the money he deceitfully earned. The story's ending reinforces the value of integrity.*)

Supplementary Activities

1. Figurative Language: Continue adding to your list. Examples: **Similes**—"he started up the street like a zombie" (p. 48); "the guitarron…was nearly as huge as a washtub" (p. 51)

2. Music: Research the differences between a guitar and a guitarron. Present your findings to the class. Use at least one visual aid in your presentation.

"Seventh Grade"

Victor, a seventh-grade student, likes a fellow classmate named Teresa. In his many efforts to get Teresa to notice him, he often scowls (a trait he learns from his best friend who assures him that scowling is a sure way to get a girl's attention) and even feigns knowing French. In the end, Teresa does notice Victor and asks him to help her study French. Fortunately for Victor, his French teacher does not tell Teresa the truth—that Victor knows next to nothing about French.

Genre: short story, young-adult fiction

Setting: Fresno, California

Point of View: third-person omniscient

Themes: young love, insecurity, fear of rejection

Conflict: person vs. self, person vs. person

Tone: conversational

Characters

Victor Rodriguez: seventh-grade boy interested in Teresa

Michael Torres: Victor's best friend; tells Victor that a great way to get a girl's attention is to constantly scowl like the guys in magazines

Teresa: girl whom Victor likes; takes notice of Victor and asks him to help her study French

Mr. Lucas: seventh-grade English teacher; teaches the class during which Victor realizes he likes Teresa

Mr. Bueller: seventh-grade French teacher; does not expose Victor's ignorance to Teresa

Vocabulary
catechism
ferocity
propelled
unison
pleaded

Discussion Questions

1. Do you think Teresa will end up liking Victor? (*Answers will vary.*)

2. What do you think of Michael's theory that girls are interested in guys who scowl? Discuss whether or not magazines are influential and if they give good information. (*Girls may be looking at Michael because they think he is good-looking, but many girls may just be wondering why he is scowling as opposed to showing interest in him. Magazines can influence people, but often their messages are not accurate. For example, many ads promote a beauty that is flawless when, in reality, beauty can be manifested in all shapes and sizes.*)

3. How do you think Victor feels when he says Teresa's name as an example of a noun in English class? Why do you think he feels this way? How might you have felt in his situation? (*Embarrassed; This makes it obvious to everyone that Teresa is on his mind. Answers will vary.*)

4. What conflict arises for Victor in French class? (*Victor claims he knows French to impress Teresa, but Mr. Bueller knows Victor is making up words. Mr. Bueller can expose Victor's lie in front of Teresa, or he can remain silent. Victor is caught in the middle of the silent struggle, hoping that Mr. Bueller will let him off the hook, which Mr. Bueller does.*)

5. Mr. Bueller does not expose Victor's lie because he remembers when he was younger and was trying to impress a girl. Discuss the concept of empathy and how it is different from sympathy. How can empathy motivate someone to be compassionate? (*Empathy means perceiving and understanding someone's emotions. Sympathy means feeling pity for someone else's misfortune. Being able to fully understand what someone is feeling makes it easier to understand his/her motivations and act in a way that is compassionate and kind toward that person.*)

Supplementary Activities

1. Figurative Language: Continue adding to your list. Examples: **Similes**—"Picking grapes was like living in Siberia, except hot and more boring" (p. 53); "[math] was confusing, like the inside of a watch" (p. 55); **Metaphors**—"rosebushes of red bloomed on Victor's cheeks" (p. 57); "a river of nervous sweat ran down his palms" (p. 57); "rosebushes of shame on his face became bouquets of love" (p. 59)

2. French: Create a glossary of basic French vocabulary that a tourist may need to use when traveling in France. When possible, also provide the pronunciation of the words in your glossary.

"Mother and Daughter"

Yollie and her mother are close, and their lives are happy. They do not have much extra money, so when Yollie needs a dress for the school dance, her mother dyes Yollie's summer dress black. Yollie is happy with her dress until she gets caught in the rain and the dye begins to run. Embarrassed, Yollie runs home and both Yollie and her mother are upset. When Yollie has a chance to go on a date with the boy she likes, Yollie's mother takes her shopping for a new outfit using a secret stash of money she has saved.

Genre: short story, young-adult fiction

Setting: Fresno, California

Point of View: third-person omniscient

Themes: young love, poverty, embarrassment

Conflict: person vs. person, person vs. nature

Tone: conversational, emotional

Characters

Yollie: eighth-grade girl; successful in school; likes Ernie

Mrs. Moreno: Yollie's mother; funny; tender-hearted toward her daughter; makes enough money to get by but is not wealthy

Ernie: boy whom Yollie likes

Janice: Yollie's best friend

Vocabulary
matinees
croquet
hassock
meager
tirade
lurched

Discussion Questions

1. Describe Yollie's relationship with her mother. (*Yollie and her mother get along well. They are friends, though it is clear that Yollie's mother is in charge. Mrs. Moreno's sense of humor makes her popular with many people, and Yollie seems to respond well to her mother's desires for her to become a successful doctor.*)
2. What do you think of Mrs. Moreno's economical solution to her daughter's problem of finding a dress for the dance? (*Answers will vary. Suggestion—The idea is clever, and Yollie is proud of her black, sophisticated dress.*)
3. Yollie is excited to dance with Ernie until she discovers the dye on her dress is running. Do you think Yollie should be embarrassed about her dress? Do you think she should have gone home or stayed at the dance? (*Yollie didn't have to be embarrassed. She could have stayed at the dance, and Ernie would probably have understood or not even noticed.*)
4. Whose fault, if anyone's, is it that Yollie's dress does not withstand the rain? How would the story be different if it had not rained at the dance? (*While Mrs. Moreno did dye the dress, it is not her fault that it was ruined by the rain. It was an unfortunate incident but nobody's fault. If it had not rained, Yollie would have felt sophisticated all night and would not have been upset about her mother's inexpensive solution to finding her a dress for the dance.*)
5. Do you think Mrs. Moreno should have used the money she is saving for Yollie's college education to buy Yollie a new outfit for her date with Ernie? Why or why not? (*Answers will*

vary. Suggestion—While the money may have been better spent on Yollie's college education, it was not a large sum of money. Mrs. Moreno obviously felt bad about Yollie's dress being ruined, and a new outfit would give a deserved boost to Yollie's pride.)

Supplementary Activities
1. Figurative Language: Continue adding to your list. Examples: **Similes**—"Yollie was slender as a tulip" (p. 62); "apples shattered like grenades" (p. 63); "the evening…like a scene from a movie" (p. 64); "dye was falling from her dress like black tears" (p. 65); **Metaphor**—"five twenties, a blossom of green that smelled sweeter than flowers" (p. 68)
2. Poetry: Write a poem that describes either the way Yollie feels while dancing with Ernie or what she feels when she discovers that the dye on her dress is running.
3. Math: Research the average cost per year of attending a state university near you. Create a pie chart that reflects how much money you think the average student pays toward his or her first year of college, including in your chart how much you think could be obtained from scholarships and loans.

"The Karate Kid"

Gilbert is inspired to take karate classes after watching the movie *The Karate Kid* and having an unfortunate run-in with the school's bully. Unfortunately, the *dojo* he attends is struggling to survive as a business, and the instructor seems to have lost his passion for karate. Because his mother invested money in the venture, Gilbert struggles through months of training, bored and uninspired, until his instructor announces that the *dojo* is closing.

Genre: short story, young-adult fiction

Setting: Fresno, California

Point of View: third-person omniscient

Themes: courage, fear, reality

Conflict: person vs. person

Tone: informative

Characters

Gilbert Sanchez: fifth-grade boy who wants to learn karate so he can defend himself against bullies

Raymundo: Gilbert's older cousin who introduces Gilbert to the movie *The Karate Kid*

Patricia: girl whom Gilbert likes

Pete the Heat: school bully; beats up Gilbert

Gilbert's mother: originally denies Gilbert's request to take karate lessons but finally gives in

Mr. Lopez: Gilbert's lackluster karate instructor

Vocabulary
perpetual
vacant
deceitful
fidgeted
reluctantly
resounded

Discussion Questions

1. In what ways is Gilbert like the Karate Kid in the movie he watches? (*He is pushed around by bullies, is polite, does his homework, keeps to himself, and wants to be strong enough to handle people who mess with him.*)

2. When Gilbert picks a fight with Pete the Heat, he is afraid. Raymundo knows he can beat up the fourth-grade bully but decides not to get involved. Do you think Raymundo should help his cousin? Explain why or why not. (*Gilbert's pride is at stake either way—either he will lose the fight to Pete or he will have to be bailed out by his older cousin. In both cases, he will not end up looking tough or capable of handling something on his own. Raymundo thinks that letting Gilbert show he has courage to fight alone is better for his cousin's image than Raymundo's coming to Gilbert's rescue.*)

3. Discuss whether or not fighting is the best way to handle a disagreement. What are other ways to resolve differences? As an example, try to come up with other ways Gilbert could have stood up to Pete cutting in line without accepting Pete's challenge to fight. (*Fighting is not the best way to handle a disagreement. Sometimes it takes as much courage to refuse a fight as to accept one. Usually, a disagreement can be resolved by talking about the situation or through compromise. Gilbert could have simply said he wouldn't fight Pete, or he could have let a teacher know about Pete's threats.*)

4. Why doesn't Gilbert's mother think Gilbert should take karate lessons? Do you think her reasons are valid? Why does she change her mind? (*She doesn't think karate will be useful to Gilbert later in life and believes Gilbert should focus on his schoolwork. While her reasons may be valid, she doesn't consider that Gilbert is pursuing an interest in something that could become a hobby and that could help him learn skills to defend himself from bullies. When she realizes that her son is getting beat up at school, and after she remembers how she felt when her parents refused to let her take dance lessons, she relents and agrees to let her son take karate lessons.*)

5. How does karate, which starts out as fascinating, become so boring to Gilbert? Why do you think Mr. Lopez is so disinterested in teaching his students karate? (*Gilbert feels like he isn't learning anything that will help him defend himself. He feels that the instructor is doing less and less to teach new skills. Mr. Lopez seems to be as bored with teaching karate as his students are of learning it. He disapproves of the fact that his students clown around, complain, are disrespectful, and don't take his instruction seriously.*)

6. Why doesn't Gilbert tell his mother about how bored he is in karate class? Do you think he should? Why or why not? (*Gilbert doesn't want his mother to think he is complaining or that she has wasted her money. He wants his mother to believe that she did the right thing in agreeing to let Gilbert take the classes. Gilbert probably should have told his mother what poor instruction he was receiving in class. Then she may have been able to talk to Mr. Lopez about improving the caliber of instruction.*)

7. Do you think Mr. Lopez made the right decision in closing the *dojo*? Why or why not? (*Answers will vary, but note that the* dojo *closing not only makes many bored students happy, but it also seems to make Mr. Lopez happy. If everyone comes away with a sense of freedom and the opportunity to perhaps do something that they may enjoy more, then it is probably a good decision.*)

Supplementary Activities
1. Figurative Language: Continue adding to your list. Examples: **Similes**—"fists were…trembling like small animals" (p. 70); "The missing component struck him like a hammer" (p. 72); "she was as nasty as a cat in a sack" (p. 79)
2. Health/Sports: On page 72, the author lists many styles of karate. Look up two different styles of karate, and compare and contrast them with each other. Present your findings in a chart or in essay form.

"La Bamba"

Manuel agrees to participate in the school's talent show by lip-synching to "La Bamba." All goes well until he realizes that dropping his record the day before caused a scratch, and the song begins to repeat itself while Manuel is onstage. At first, Manuel feels embarrassed but later is surprised and pleased when he receives compliments on his funny performance.

Genre: short story, young-adult fiction

Setting: Fresno, California

Point of View: third-person omniscient

Themes: courage, fame, fear of rejection

Conflict: person vs. self

Tone: informative, descriptive

Characters

Manuel Gomez: fifth-grade boy who offers to participate in the school talent show

Benny: trumpet player in the school talent show whose loud trumpet blow causes Manuel to drop his record during the show's dress rehearsal

Mr. Roybal: the school's talent coordinator

Vocabulary
limelight
pantomime
debut
hygiene
ado
verge

Discussion Questions
1. Why does Manuel think the night of the talent show will be a night to remember? *(He is excited to be in the limelight, and he looks forward to his brothers and sisters being jealous and pouting because Manuel will receive so much attention from their parents.)*
2. Do you think, as Manuel does, that everything will go smoothly for his performance in the talent show? Why or why not? *(Answers will vary, but note that earlier the author may have foreshadowed a problem when the record player Mr. Roybal uses does not work properly with Manuel's record.)*
3. What is your impression of the talent show? *(Answers will vary.)*
4. What does Manuel do to get the audience excited about his performance? What do you think it takes to be a good entertainer? *(Manuel begins doing fancy dance steps. Suggested answers—having a good personality, being humorous, or being a good singer, dancer, etc.)*

5. Why is Manuel embarrassed by the needle sticking when everyone else thinks he does an excellent job? (*Manuel is embarrassed because he knows that the needle was not intended to stick and thinks that everyone else knows as well. However, the audience is unaware that Manuel did not plan the mishap. Because they think the "accident" was intentional, they find it funny and entertaining.*)

6. Do you think Manuel will volunteer to be in the talent show the next year? Why or why not? (*Answers will vary.*)

Supplementary Activities
1. Figurative Language: Continue adding to your list. Examples: **Similes**—"applause as loud as a thunderstorm" (p. 81); "hiss that sounded like a snake" (p. 82); "raised his hand like a symphony conductor" (p. 83); "watching him, like they would a monkey at the zoo" (p. 86); "he shivered and snaked like Michael Jackson" (p. 87); "sheets were as cold as the moon" (p. 89)

2. Science: With a teacher or parent's assistance, recreate the light bulb science experiment Manuel describes on pages 83–84. Present the experiment to the class.

"The Marble Champ"

Lupe Medrano is good at everything academic but is not good at anything athletic. Desiring to win a competition based on physical activity, she decides to try her hand at marbles and practices intently for the upcoming marble competition. In the end, Lupe wins the entire competition, not only beating out the other girl competitors but also the boys' champion.

Genre: short story, young-adult fiction

Setting: Fresno, California

Point of View: third-person omniscient

Themes: victory, determination, goals

Conflict: person vs. person, person vs. self

Tone: informative, descriptive

Characters

Lupe Medrano: 12-year-old girl; excellent student but wants to be good at something athletic, as well

Mr. and Mrs. Medrano: Lupe's parents; supportive of her endeavor to become a marble champion

Alfonso: neighborhood marble champion; helps Lupe train for her competition

Rachel, Yolanda, and Miss Baseball Cap: three of the girls Lupe beats on her way to winning the marble championship

Vocabulary
rummaged
accurate
agate
quivering
opponent
commotion

Discussion Questions

1. Why do you think it is important to Lupe to be good at some kind of sport? (*Because Lupe is ambitious, it may be that she wants to tackle the one thing she has not yet mastered. Or, she may feel that her other achievements aren't as exciting because they came more easily to her. Perhaps she wants the satisfaction of winning something that will require more effort than her academic work does.*)

2. Do you think that Lupe will do well at the marble championship? Why or why not? (*Answers will vary, but note that Lupe diligently practices and trains. However, while she is teachable, she has never demonstrated particularly great athletic skill in any type of sport.*)

3. In her pursuit of winning the marble championship, Lupe is fighting two battles. Identify the two forms of conflict and whether or not Lupe wins the battles. (*Lupe is fighting against herself [person vs. self] to prove she can excel at something that is not academic and that does not come naturally. Lupe is also competing against other people who are skilled at playing marbles [person vs. person]. By beating her competitors, Lupe wins her battle against others and herself. She proves to herself that she can win an award for a sport.*)

4. Discuss how hard Lupe works to achieve her goal of winning the marble championship. How important is faithful, dedicated practice to achieving a goal? (*Discussions will vary. Lupe practices many hours every day and strengthens her thumb to the point that people think her large muscle is evidence of a broken or disjointed thumb. Practicing is usually a very large part of what makes a person successful at achieving a goal like Lupe's.*)

5. **Prediction:** Do you predict that Lupe will ever enter another physical-type competition again? Why do you think so?

Supplementary Activities

1. Figurative Language: Continue adding to your list. Example: **Simile**—"her thumb was weaker than the neck of a newborn chick" (p. 91)

2. Art: Draw a caricature of Lupe playing marbles. Be sure to emphasize her thumb, which onlookers think is broken before Lupe begins to play.

3. Journal: In your journal, write your thoughts about good sportsmanship. What does it take to be a good sport, and what is the value in it?

"Growing Up"

Maria doesn't want to go on vacation with her family, so she stays home with her grandmother. However, feeling guilty for talking disrespectfully to her father, Maria spends her week alone worrying about the well-being of her parents and siblings. When they return home full of grand tales and stories of fun adventures, Maria is jealous of the fun they had while she spent so much time worrying about them. She takes back all of her promises to be nice to her family but finally realizes she would rather be with them than without them.

Genre: short story, young-adult fiction

Setting: Fresno, California

Point of View: third-person omniscient

Themes: coming-of-age, family, loneliness, guilt, jealousy

Conflict: person vs. person, person vs. self

Tone: descriptive, introspective

Characters

Maria: tenth-grade girl who does not want to go on summer vacation with her family

Irma, Rudy, and John: Maria's younger sister and brothers

Rafael: Maria's father; hard-working man who grew up in Mexico

Eva: Maria's mother; tries to be sensitive to Maria's needs as she grows older

Grandmother Lupe: Maria's "nina," with whom she stays while her family is on vacation

Becky: Maria's friend

Vocabulary
trinkets
foreman
dilute
trellis
miffed

Discussion Questions

1. The author lists many reasons why Maria is dissatisfied with her family's vacations. What do you think motivates Maria to want to stay home this year? (*Maria wants to be a bit more independent and feels too grown up to go on family vacations. She also mentions how boring it can get sitting around while the adults talk. Maria describes how she felt poor at Disneyland last year because of the way she was dressed.*)

2. Maria is tired of her father's stories about Mexico. Why do you suppose parents sometimes tell their children stories about their own childhoods? (*Parents want their children to appreciate what they have and the hard work it took to make their lives possible, especially parents who had to overcome significant obstacles to find success or freedom—financial or otherwise.*)

3. Do you think Maria would be so paranoid about something happening to her family if she had not had a fight with her father before they left? (*Her fear is likely due to the guilt she feels for telling her family to go without her and for being rude to her father. However, she may have also worried about them even if her father left on good terms with her. Simply being away from her family could have made her nervous about their well-being.*)

4. Why does Maria's attitude about her family change so quickly after they return home? Why does she take back all of her promises? Is she being reasonable or not? Explain. (*Maria is upset that her family had fun while she spent the entire vacation worrying about them. She also feels jealous that they had so much fun without her. Her irritation that they had a good time makes her feel justified in taking back her promises. She doesn't have to worry anymore, because they have all arrived home safely. Maria is not being reasonable, and she realizes this when she declares, "Something's wrong with me" [p. 107].*)

5. What are some universal elements that the author includes in this short story for his young readers? (*Examples—Maria fights with her father, and many teenagers fight with their parents. Maria is upset when her brothers and sisters have fun without her, and many siblings experience some form of sibling rivalry. Maria is tired of her parents' stories and can't wait to move out of the house, and many teenagers feel the same way as they begin to feel more capable and independent.*)

Supplementary Activities

1. Figurative Language: Continue adding to your list. Example: **Metaphor**—"letting anxiety eat a hole in her soul" (p. 105)

2. Journal: In your journal, write about where you would go for your dream vacation. What would you do there? Use descriptive language when describing your dream vacation.

3. Writing: Maria is worried that something may have happened to her family on their way to San Jose. Compose a letter that a worried Maria might send to her parents while they are on vacation.

Post-reading Discussion Questions

1. Gary Soto has been lauded for writing universal stories to which everyone can relate. Do you agree or disagree that his stories are relatable? (*Even though all of the stories are about Latino teenagers who live in a specific part of California, the emphasis of the stories has more to do with the children's emotions, insecurities, fears, and dreams than their culture or socioeconomic status. In this way, young readers need not identify with characters' cultural or socioeconomic identities as much as their emotions or the way they respond to different situations. Also note that the story's pop culture references are outdated, but even so, readers can still relate to the characters because the references are peripheral to the actual story.*)

2. What are some common threads you discovered about short stories from reading *Baseball in April and Other Stories*? (*All of the stories develop a main character almost immediately, and in most stories, the character evolves very little from beginning to end. The conflicts are always very easy to understand and are resolved fairly quickly. Vivid description is important so that the author can help the reader understand the characters more easily. While each story's plot and characters are unique, each story focuses on a snapshot of a person's life with the intent of capturing a moment that caused that character to grow or learn something s/he did not understand before.*)

3. What are some specific types of information that Soto gives to readers early in the stories to set up the plots and develop the characters? (*He gives ages, grades, descriptions of physical features, descriptions of personalities, a breakdown of a main character's family, and descriptions of each story's setting.*)

4. What do you think of Soto's incorporating Spanish phrases into his writing? Did these phrases add or detract from the story? (*Answers will vary. Understanding these phrases may have proven difficult at times, but some students may speak and understand Spanish. Still others may have enjoyed learning something new. The phrases added to the story by making it more realistic, as kids in Fresno may talk this way. However, the phrases may detract from the story by making it harder for some students to understand.*)

5. What are some major themes that surface in multiple stories in the book? (*Suggestions—courage, acceptance, fear [especially fear of rejection], family, friendship, disappointment, dreams, success/failure*)

6. What messages do you think the author wants readers to take away from the book? (*Answers will vary. Suggestion—The author wants children to understand that they can learn things from everyone and that people are more similar than they might think. Money, age, and culture may play a part in a person's life, but the reality is that everyone faces challenges, everyone must grow up, and this process is not always easy.*)

7. Would you recommend this book to a friend? Why or why not? (*Answers will vary.*)

Post-reading Extension Activities

1. Writing: Select one short story. Write a second short story about what happens next in the main character's life.
2. Writing: Write a poem about a topic to which you think your peers could relate. Include at least two Spanish phrases from the book's glossary.
3. Art: Create a diorama that depicts one of the short stories' central conflicts.
4. Art: Draw a caricature of your favorite character from the book.
5. Oral Presentation: Just like Manuel in "La Bamba," determine a talent you have, and showcase it for your class.
6. Writing/Drama: Turn one of the short stories into a play. Form a group, write the script based on the dialogue in the story, assign roles, and perform the play for the class.
7. Literary Analysis: Complete the Story Map found on page 28 of this guide for at least two short stories in the book.

Assessment for *Baseball in April and Other Stories*

Assessment is an ongoing process. The following nine items can be completed during study of the novel. Once finished, the student and teacher will check the work. Points may be added to indicate the level of understanding.

Name _____ Date _____

Student	Teacher	
_____	_____	1. Correct all quizzes and tests taken over the book.
_____	_____	2. Write summaries of two short stories. Use at least five vocabulary words in each of your summaries.
_____	_____	3. Complete the Character Web on page 29 of this guide for the main character in one of the stories.
_____	_____	4. Identify at least four conflicts characters in the stories face; then use these to complete the Conflict Chart on page 30 of this guide. (The conflicts may come from more than one short story.)
_____	_____	5. In a paragraph, explain why Soto's book is considered to have universal appeal to young readers.
_____	_____	6. Complete two Post-reading Extension Activities, and present them to the class.
_____	_____	7. Write a letter to Gary Soto explaining what you think of his book of short stories.
_____	_____	8. Write an essay that compares and contrasts two main characters from different stories.
_____	_____	9. Using a problem from one of the stories in the book, complete the Decision-making Grid on page 31 of this guide.

Novel and Short Story

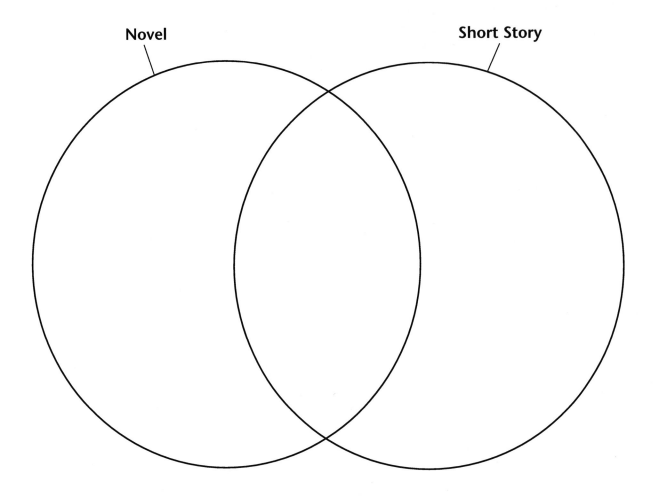

Pros and Cons

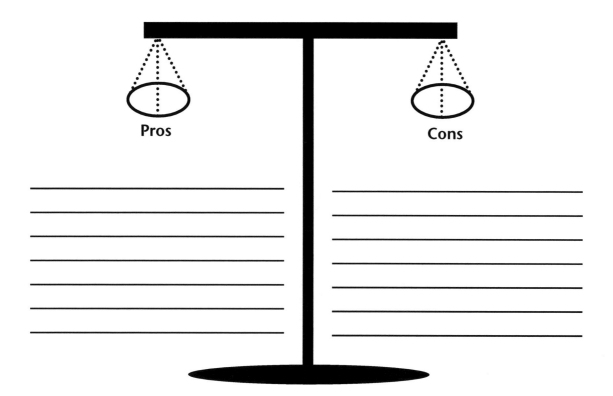

Story Map

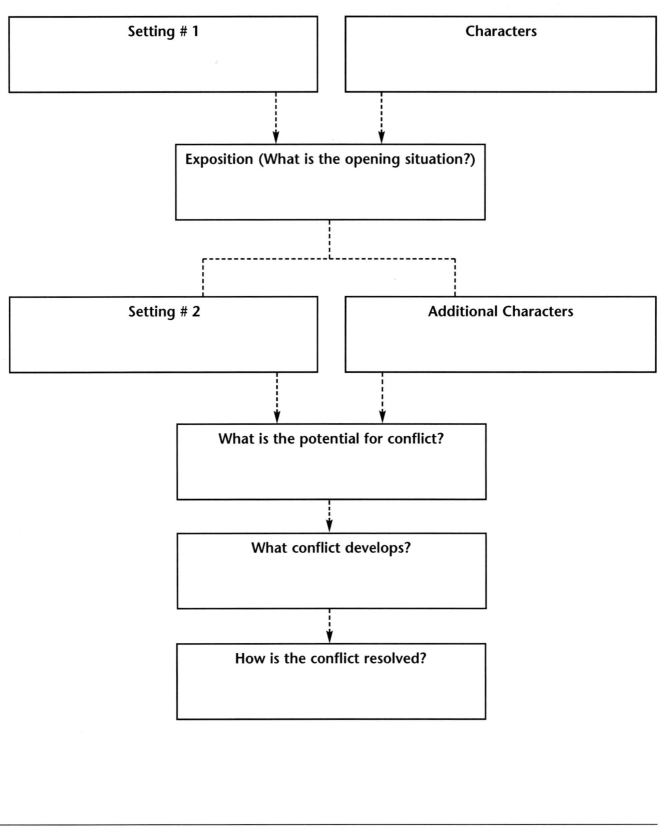

Character Web

Directions: Complete the attribute web by filling in information specific to a character in the book.

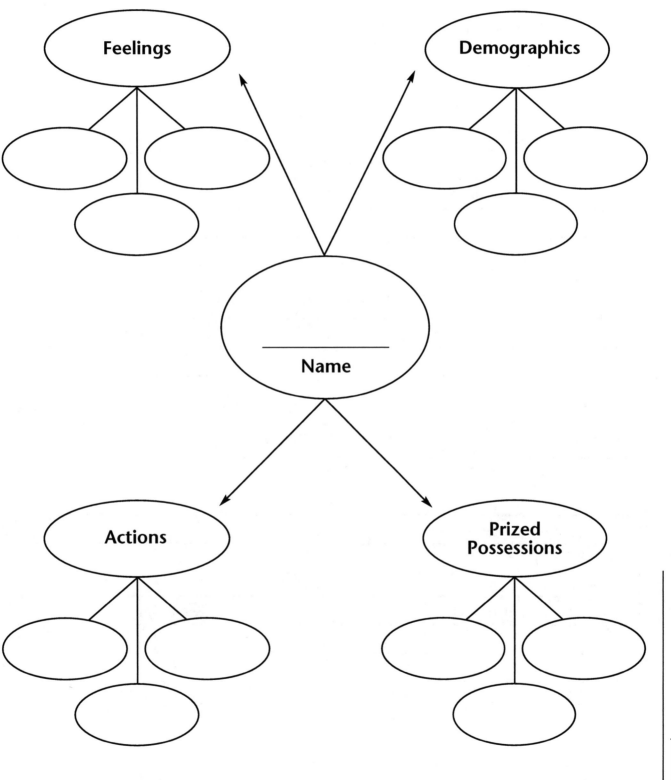

Conflict

The **conflict** of a story is the struggle between two people or two forces. There are four main types of conflict: person vs. person, person vs. nature, person vs. society, and person vs. self.

Directions: In the space provided, list four conflicts a character experiences and justify why you identify it with that particular type of conflict. Then explain how each conflict is resolved in the story.

person vs. person

Conflict	Resolution

person vs. nature

Conflict	Resolution

person vs. society

Conflict	Resolution

person vs. self

Conflict	Resolution

Decision-making Grid

Directions: The decision-making grid below is supposed to make it easier to find the best solution to a problem. Fill in criterion #3 with another question you believe is important to ask when making a decision. Then fill in the grid. Choose a solution and write a paragraph explaining the reasons behind your choice.

	Criterion #1	Criterion #2	Criterion #3
State the problem:	Will the solution hurt someone?	Will it make me feel better?	
Solution #1:			
Solution #2:			
Solution #3:			
Solution #4:			

Linking Novel Units® Lessons to National and State Reading Assessments

During the past several years, an increasing number of students have faced some form of state-mandated competency testing in reading. Many states now administer state-developed assessments to measure the skills and knowledge emphasized in their particular reading curriculum. The discussion questions and post-reading questions in this Novel Units® Teacher Guide make excellent open-ended comprehension questions and may be used throughout the daily lessons as practice activities. The rubric below provides important information for evaluating responses to open-ended comprehension questions. Teachers may also use scoring rubrics provided for their own state's competency test.

Please note: The Novel Units® Student Packet contains optional open-ended questions in a format similar to many national and state reading assessments.

Scoring Rubric for Open-Ended Items

3-Exemplary
Thorough, complete ideas/information
Clear organization throughout
Logical reasoning/conclusions
Thorough understanding of reading task
Accurate, complete response

2-Sufficient
Many relevant ideas/pieces of information
Clear organization throughout most of response
Minor problems in logical reasoning/conclusions
General understanding of reading task
Generally accurate and complete response

1-Partially Sufficient
Minimally relevant ideas/information
Obvious gaps in organization
Obvious problems in logical reasoning/conclusions
Minimal understanding of reading task
Inaccuracies/incomplete response

0-Insufficient
Irrelevant ideas/information
No coherent organization
Major problems in logical reasoning/conclusions
Little or no understanding of reading task
Generally inaccurate/incomplete response